FINISHING LINE PRESS

www.finishinglinepress.com

lowercase aesthetic

poems by

riley p. murdock

Finishing Line Press
Georgetown, Kentucky

lowercase aesthetic

ACKNOWLEDGMENTS

to Cristina, for forcing me to work on this and for being my first audience. I love you more than anything.

to mom, dad, Conner, Ethan, Ashley and the numerous members of my family for being wonderful always.

to Jamie, Cam, Allie Cat and Murphy for giving me a home away from home during quarantine.

to Stretch, for being the absolute best and for keeping me company the night i couldn't sleep and stayed up way too late editing the first draft of this. i will always love you.

to Moose, for filling a cat-sized hole in my heart, ya goof.

to Salem, for appearing into our lives out of nowhere like a floofy love missile.

to Winston, for being a constant, warm, squeaky presence in my adult life that i will miss dearly.

to Finnegan, for being a very, very good boy.

to Divya, for pushing me out of my comfort zone and helping me look at my work critically.

to Robin, for your kindness, guidance, and encouragement.

to Grace and Alexis, for inspiring me to take this leap.

to Grandma & Grandpa Murdock, Eva, Katie, Eric, Patrick, Karma, Jack, and Bob: thank you for the love you left in my life and the lives of others. i miss you.

to everyone who is reading this right now: thank you. it really means a lot that you bothered to support me, whether you end up enjoying this book or not.

Publisher: Leah Huete de Maines
Editor: Christen Kincaid
Cover Art and Design: Riley Murdock
Author Photo: Anntaninna Biondo

Order online: www.finishinglinepress.com
also available on amazon.com

Author inquiries and mail orders:
Finishing Line Press
PO Box 1626
Georgetown, Kentucky 40324
USA

contents

part iii:

part iv:

part i.

'untitled' is still a title

i can't describe what it is.
a sound, a smell, some sense
that only exists between synapses
it gravitates me toward
hot showers
late at night
and early morning drives
where just a hint of today's
light peeks around the corner.
drives, yes, at night
with a song that perfectly fits the hour
looking down at city lights
drives from the back seat,
daydreaming about the trains
on the way to my cousins' old house
a hoodie and a football
a michigan fall
you can almost taste the air
like a sommelier
huffing the most potent
cellar cabernet
but in the opposite way,
faint and undetected
like smelling a lacroix

that feeling
hugs my soul
it aches the way love does
when it's young
(at least at heart)
it's total
the way a cat trusts.
the way a memory tangles itself inside you
like putting off sleep
with soft music and just the right headspace
like gentle, pressing weight
when it's not too warm for blankets

america's backyard

in march 2020,
all signs pointed to lauderdale.
surrounded by close friends,
i waited to enter a crowded bar, thinking
it would be nice if the line was shorter
so we could be inside.
the monkey's paw curled
and so did millions.

love, part i: prose-colored glasses

old hurt
sewn into the fabrics
of the soul,
a quilt patched together
with memories, the pain cut out.
fallen to the floor, empty pieces of
tape
that fill in backstory
the test audiences considered extraneous. there is something beautiful
about how we are all pulled
toward melancholy. a cholera
sometimes lethal, often crippling
when we recover, it calls
from a phone booth, in the rain
surrounded by the dark begging us to come outside.
our lungs long for tar even as they gasp
and wilt.

addicted to the aesthetic
of lowercase letters

our lives spent writing unsent texts, then
holding backspace

dawn of the second day

—48 hours remain—

(pov: you are working from home. it's raining outside and you're
nostalgic for the time you spent as a child playing *the legend of zelda:
majora's mask* in your grandmother's basement. you are listening to
clock town day 2. you associate this song with the comfort you now
find in thunder.)

my eyes open from black sleep
to bustle and birds chirping.
rain on the window
the damp soaks into me
while i stay dry.
in my head there's sunlight
the world wakes
for the second time
and the millionth and one
plus-one.
the damp boardwalk smells
like vhs tapes sound
when rewinding.
like a crtv's buzz
like midwestern dew
on midwestern eyes.
on a morning like this
you almost remember
all the times the world
has met with a terrible

fate.
and will again.
haven't we?
a million deaths and rebirths
dripping down the windows
and one cup of coffee
dripping down the soul.
i long for these moments between
assignment and deadline
opportunity and obligation

freedom and responsibility
start and end
tranquility and disaster
genesis and revelations
the morning has begun
the ending is yet to come.

midnight oil

my darling, the night burns
not of city lights,
incandescent, iridescent
shimmering through the streets,
but of longing in my chest.
your hair is not there
to bandage my wounds.

ouroboros

~~dishes~~
~~laundry~~
meditate
~~8 hours of work~~
8 hours of sleep? never
8 hours of recreation?
remember to eat make coffee
write it down before you forget
~~...shit~~
8 hours of choosing,
by not choosing,
to do nothing
pulled like a rope between
the sink
and the keyboard
neither, nor me
in motion
because we have not
been acted upon.
(ad-lib: first law!)
~~at rest~~ but never resting
~~at work~~ but never working ~~lying down~~ but never sleeping
~~reading endlessly~~ but never reading
~~dishes~~
~~laundry~~
meditate

a flat circle

i.
i wear a shirt
from time to time
put together long
before i was
commemorating a race
my father ran
before my older brother
had a single cell
since it's been mine,
it's yellowed slightly.
one sleeve refuses to give
any slack to my wrist.
there are small holes in
a few places.
big enough for concern,
small enough to get by
mostly unseen.

ii.
i swear at a cat
from time to time.
hissing back in retaliation
and flattery.
once she might have been
sweet, even loving.
now she seems
to resent more than
a moment of my attention
with teeth and tongue.
my brother loves her
more than anything.
they can pester her
with love, with mischief
and she will rarely
ever complain.
the big sister
they never had,
a small companion
put together long
before they were.

catsong

like clockwork, allie cat
will wind up and chime
chittering in an imitation
of birdsong
as she longingly stares
out the window.

this apex predator
separated from its prey
cannot help but sing
of its majesty.
the birds
cannot hear.

i love you, cat

why are you biting me
stop

toy story

once you learn your playthings are people
you start to understand them.
you wonder how that bionicle you couldn't wait for feels
now that you haven't seen it in a decade.

you find yourself in the socks at the back of the drawer,
you feel for the tupperwares and bowls
that stay at the bottom of the stack
looking up while the ones at the top get picked
over and over

who are you to leave them alone like this?
who are you to act like you never knew them?
you know the golden rule.

you know you would shrivel if you were the last apple left,
picked up and turned over and prodded, each suitor
finding each bruise and soft spot, every crater
knowing another, less-flawed, was next door

paper

is alive
you can do whatever you want with it you can stretch it you can
betray
it you can bend it to your will you can tear
it in half.
you can love it you can
leave it to
rot
alone or in broken company
let it tumble down the street, dirtied by
sleet
paint it gray. feed it to the
dirt
or through a shredder
or through your mouth
you can stroke it
cut your fingers on the
ends
share your deepest pains and greatest
joys your highest hopes and lowest
fears
hold it close
to your heart and beg
it not to crumple
from the pressure of
your arms.

ii.
i have birthed many
love letters
the first few
i was not ready
to be a father for.
years ago
i went out for cigarettes
and burned them.

hardened (the first crime)

i committed my first offense (to my knowledge)
at my grandmother's house.
i was seven or some other dumbfuck age
i did not understand that "hard" meant that there was alcohol in that
tasty looking lemonade. i was thirsty
and i was seven.

what i did understand,
and knew for certain once an adult realized what i'd done,
is when that half a fluid ounce of 5%
hit my tongue and i had officially mipped,
it was only a matter of time before they found me. the cops were
already on the way. they knew.

that evening (or one of many others spent there at some other
dumbfuck age)
i had admonished a friend of my cousin for smoking
that's bad for you, i had learned.
how the tables turn, you little fucking narc.

(of a plant or fruit) young or unripe

i once stood
beside a staircase
beside myself,
angry that I picked yellow
to be my favorite color
over green
as if it were a marriage vow.

i was green
my world was camping trips where the sunrise
painted a gradient
the water, the moss
the trees
flowing in different shades.
freshly shorn grass all cut by my father
to an equal length
when his hair was still brown.

the drab shade my car wears
the leaves that tunnel me in
as i leave home.
the road brown and pocked
until it is asphalt

we are green until we wake up gray.

part ii.

you are michigan

the weather isn't always kind to you
but beneath the extra layers,
your heart is never hidden.
your mood's never far from a bonfire
cooking smores at all times in your mind
sometimes the leaves fall too soon
sometimes the winter stays too long.
the conversation moves from the living room
to the front door
to the cars. eventually the hugs end
and we drive away, pausing thrice to wave and smile

spring will come, tax season with it
death someday.
but whether it's the great lakes in the air,
in the clouds, on the plows or at the beach
i am *alive* in your every season.
you are an oversized hoodie and gym shorts,
you're crocs in the snow.
you're drive-thru coney dogs,
you're the unstoppable tide of square pizza.
you're the unbreakable spirit of lions,
you're the immortal, undead faith that this is their year.
you're you and that lets me be me
two puzzles we can work on together,
especially when it gets dark and rainy.
i'll never tire of the landscapes
they depict.

(i refuse to compare you to potholes.)

money crusher go brrr (the second crime)

my next offense
was first degree murder
of the president of the united states.
i crushed abraham lincoln's skull
on a railroad track
just to watch him shine.
i was probably 10 or some other dumbfuck age.

you see, it was fun to intentionally destroy u.s. currency.
by that point i was a career criminal. i didn't give a fuck
that it was only a matter of time
before the law caught up with me. i just wanted
to eat some superman ice cream on a humid
harrisville evening, mood-lit by fireflies
and the town's only stoplight
and watch
a john wilkes caboose sic semper tyransform honest abe's face into a
formless void.

i had killed the only thing worth less than an opinion. the authorities
turned a blind eye. i stashed the evidence
in a leather-bound collection of trophies
made from the corpses of similar victims.

(for legal purposes, obviously
i am referring to crushing pennies)

deficit

adhd is fun because
you can be doing really well at managing it,
only forgetting the occasional meeting
gainfully employed, in a healthy relationship
and every few months your wallet or keys will vanish
into thin air
taking with them every minute spent
listening to podcasts, meditating,
setting reminders
reminding yourself that you're not a fuck up

you'll call yourself an irredeemable, unfathomable moron
an utterly miserable failure of a human being
a pathetic waste of neurons, fat and veins
and you will believe it.

if you find them,
and that's a big if
it will either be after changing your locks
ordering a new driver's license
and freezing your accounts
or in the dumbest, most obvious place imaginable
or both.

(after writing this, it was revealed
that my keys were in her purse
the whole time
and i hated myself for no reason.
i will learn nothing from this experience)

the rng chose shania

and she's not happy about it
but that's damn sure what she's gonna read

when i was driving earlier today, she told me,
it occurred to me that it was the first time in years
i was driving and actually cared whether
i survived the trip. before it was 'ehhhh?', she said,
gesturing her hand like an uneven desk.

i tell her she doesn't have to read shania tonight if she doesn't want to. that
doing things we don't enjoy isn't worth spending our unpaid hours
but the rng chose shania
and that choice was final.

i make so many decisions during the day, she said, sleep in her voice
sometimes i just want the decisions made for me.

okay then, i say, you're reading toni morrison tonight. there.
decision made.

but the rng chose shania
and that's who she's choosing

dream signs

"dreams in general seem like life, with certain notable exceptions."
—stephen laberge

many nights i find myself bonded
with cats i don't recognize.
its never ones i know
but i do know them,
as long as i'm asleep.

they lead me to new landscapes. adventures
new worlds hidden around the corner
sometimes they will find danger
evil,
violence
and i will run after them
screaming
without sound, a muted croak
chords in shock, paralyzed
by one half of the brain,
the other choking
on a fictional infinity.

...
*(crissy wakes up suddenly. i'm raising my voice in my sleep. the words
aren't words. the panic is real. she gently rouses me. you were yelling, she
says. i apologize, wondering why
my voice fails the vulnerable in my mind
and torments those i love
outside it)*
...

many nights i find myself singing
at the top of my lungs
voice warmed and clear,
air abundant. projection effortless
imaginary diaphragm, real joy
the plot doesn't matter, where i'm at
is not matter. nor are
these people. my tones do not shake
any molecules.
my head is a car and
the windows are up

rem

pulled into pieces i
stagger through the fragments
my thoughts cracked,
my memory serrated
i sing
at the top of my lungs
i marvel
at the violence of it all.
here is the universe! i belt,
here we are truly alone!

laika

like a dog
floating
free
in an
ocean of
stars
i am
surrounded
by wonder
and
suffocating

my hands

are fine
right where they are,
thank you.
entwined
behind and
under
my head,
they cannot pick or scratch or twist or pull or bleed
they cannot
be bitten

ii.
torn cuticles don't inspire symphonies.
shakespeare, to my knowledge, never once
composed
a sonnet about how lovingly
his couch held him.

makeout reef

my tongue is fat
a clumsy, graceless blob
disrespectful of its surroundings,
always running into walls.
it fidgets with spit
picks at the gap
beneath my concave
low incisors
until the sounds drive you batshit.

yours is lithe
fluid and flexible
i've seen it dance, lengthen out
its partner a smile,
it's routine well-rehearsed
executed flawlessly.

mine prefers the feel
of your teeth,
held tight in a breathless embrace
it has two left feet but
yours laughs and twirls,
convinced mine can learn to match
the sway of its hips.

tgif

oh fuck yeah its *friday night*
we're gonna get *litty*
i might even go as far as to
lay down and look at my phone for six hours.
i'm the life of the party

i am the wojak standing in the corner
thinking *they don't know how lonely i feel*
as i scroll and scroll
~~making friends~~ acquainting myself with reddit randos
smiling and politely nodding while
listening in on their conversations
like i'm in the dmz between two topics
at a dinner table.
(smiling and nodding) :||

still better than leaving the house. or doing anything
i couldn't immediately decide to stop doing.

i want so badly to do everything
except anything.

i make the grandest plans for these
nights when you are away.
i'll record songs, write stories
fix the house, devour novels
but the moment you walk out the door,
i search my beard for any hairs
you may have left there.
i relive years of solitude, periods of break
followed by long stretches of ache. all the
times that broken clocks were right
until i found you.

you are gravity
you are air.
you are food and water,
you are shelter.

arms

can hold
and strangle.
arms can be home they can pull
close that which you love and
smother
always with you
right there left there making trouble
saying goodbye
and hello and fuck you
and blowing kisses.
they come equipped
with handy tools
for lying loving
and knitting.
these ten wonderful appendages come standard
the dealer package includes an upgrade
to weaponry.
arms can persuade
better than a mouth.
arms can race better than legs.
and they can fall
they can hold
up

six minutes

(for emma gonzalez)

i did not ask to be here.
i did not ask to stand in front of this crowd
i did not ask for you to wait on my words.
i did beg for my life
for six minutes.

yet, they see fit to shoot at us
with vitriol
so others may shoot at us
with powder and lead.
a lethal cash injection
delivered at 3,300 feet per second
date of transaction:
2/14/18
they would gladly have pulled the trigger themselves
if bullets would purchase my silence.
       rend my lips
       twist teeth from my mouth,
       as they exit my throat.
       laughing at my mangled face
       as cries of pain fell
       on deaf ears.
       and,
raising their fists triumphant,
       bellowing with pride and rage
       before the cartridge hit the tile,
       they would tell the world i deserved it:
       a preemptive strike the only way
       to stop a deranged youth.
the only thing that can stop a bad guy with a machine is a good girl
with a mouth.
and six minutes.
six minutes where i will give them what they want
and they will tremble like the thunder
of 150 shots tearing
twisting
rending
us.

of 180 unfired, their purpose snuffed
like the dead.
left adorned with swastikas
as if to tell them, like our crosses do
we will return to dust.
and they call *me* skinhead.

for six minutes they will tremble
scared shitless of 17 voices
now forever silent.
though i will not speak
i will roar.

2/14/23

(five years later, when a mass shooter killed three students at the same campus where i wrote six minutes)

what's worse,
outrage at the outrageous
or stomping onto a soap box of dead kids
and declaring that you don't give a shit,
that the status quo is more valuable than the corpses
that wear bullet holes
and the treads of your boots

you are lower than the lowest. i would
dehumanize you but
that'd be an insult to insects.
you've proven we can be so much worse

part iii.

4:04 a.m.

i am a blue screen
staring at a blue screen
frozen

this is the rabbit hole
the portal, the fire pole
sliding down the ego to the id
a pill crawling down the throat

crossed on this shit
potent as hell
hating today
dreading tomorrow

dead sea, doomscroll
lurking in the depths
the void calling from the comment section
knowing there's no air
inhaling all the same

eyes scorched with blue
receptors gorged
hating today
fighting off tomorrow

meditating on dead dreams
of making the world care about
anything at all,
much less you.

addicted to the aesthetic of
lowercase letters

tolerating today
raging against tomorrow

you can't run away

from the world.
every step you take
it walks with you.
no matter how high you build
your roots will twist
beneath the ground.
ignorant speck.

feedback loop

all i create
are quantum particles
changing states
at the thought of being
observed

deciding to eat the cheese straight out of the bag because why not? who's going to stop me? i do what i want

"jesus christ, i'm 26." —dan "soupy" campbell

we watch as a grown, adult male human
stalks his prey. there's only one way
this can end, folks: carnage.

see him stumble shiftily to the front of the fridge
search his surroundings to ensure he's
alone. time to advance
he creeps forward, creaks open the door
reaches in, and ! just like that, rips open the
drawer in the bottom left. exposing
the sustenance in its abdomen.
he gleefully removes a glistening pouch, tears it open
and, with his bare hands
takes his prize, the golden strands of heaven:
shredded cheese. the four cheese mexican
blend, to be precise. his favorite.
he has seized his kill.

having eaten his fill,
he slinks away into silence
his cravings sated
his independence asserted,
undetected among the living.

an ode to reddit

friends have come
mostly gone
days have blurred and mingled and romanced
a perfect pair of years coasting by
content with comfort and unconcerned
about the weather.

hundreds of nights spent
inside walls both physical
and mental and chemical
and rectangular and bright

what we don't experience
we read
what we don't see
we feel
millions of words
poured from millions of souls
life, distilled
into pixels.

searching the heavens for the phone i just put down

when we lose our minds
where do they go?

do they tour oblivion,
stay in a hostel with guitar picks
go biking with car keys
and remote controls?

are they on vacation somewhere,
clinking glasses with elvis,
jim morrison, d.b. cooper
and the wmds?

are they in a pocket dimension,
chilling
next to what you planned to do before
walking through that door frame?

are they hopelessly
lost in the countryside,
stubbornly refusing to just ask someone for some goddamn directions
already
like a fucking adult?

are they doomed for the incinerator,
ending in fire like all things
destined to mix ashes
with their long-dead memories?

mipped again (the third crime)

i drank an *irish car bomb* with my aunt
that was pretty cool

russian blue

stretch is a cat
stretch is deaf
stretch likes to stretch.
stretch is a little stretch that does a big stretch.
stretch has very long arms.
etymologists believe his name originated from this behavior roughly 4 months
b.a.
stretch struts with one foot way out in front at a time. stretch gives em the ol
razzle dazzle.
stretch will stretch him little paw out to touch his people.

stretch loves his people.
stretch likes to wake up from deep naps, dreaming of second scoops, to find
his people approaching.
stretch likes to acknowledge his people by throwing his head back slightly,
opening his mouth as if to talk without speaking. because we see it, he knows
we don't need to hear it because he doesn't. i do it back.
stretch greets his people with an affectionate nudge
or a firm headbutt. he thinks smashing his face into you is
a declaration of true love.
stretch whistles in his sleep. stretch breathes out through his lips and the
sputter of his depressurization is audible through the room.
stretch does not know he whistles in his sleep.
stretch does not know he whistles.

stretch rumbles. stretch is set to tumble dry low in 10 minute cycles.

stretch screeches. stretch is set to max volume and his closed captioning is
several seconds behind.
stretch's audio is mixed very low for dialogue scenes and like a rick rubin
metallica album for action sequences.

stretch is an impulse purchase
stretch is all our best impulses wrapped in fur and delivered to our doorstep.

stretch was found with a broken leg.
he came home with a fresh shave down the buttocks.
stretch asked us to delete photos of this. we have no comment

stretch has a queen-size bed to himself.
on that bed, stretch likes to lay on my guitar.
off that bed, stretch likes to lay in a basket
or on top of a knit mat strategically placed atop his cat tree for optimal
birdwatching
(stretch is a member of the audubon society)
or on my dirty clothes.

stretch is an immensely stressed animal
which he shows constantly
by splaying out, belly exposed
eyes shut tight. ears not twitching
teef bared
his one white toe in the air

stretch has two homes, one for work and one for vacations. he likes to invite
his grandparents to his vacation home. he also shares it with his uncle jack, a
toasted bagel raised by cats who was eager to teach him in the ancient arts of
begging.

stretch is locked in a custody battle with his grandmother, who often attempts
to abduct him.

stretch loves his momma lap, preferably marinated in fuzzy blanket and
sometimes cooked over heating pad.
stretch likes to make biscuits to go with his meals. stretch's biscuits are
delicious enough to cause ratatouille flashbacks and entrance one in faint,
comfortable nostalgia of early childhood, reminiscing of a place and time,
conveniently dated to when you grew up, in which the world was objectively
simpler and kinder.

stretch mounts his litter box like captain morgan on a barrel
eternally channeling hans zimmer with every bathroom break
meowmeow meow meow, meowmeow meow meow, meowmeow meow
meow, meowmeoemeowmeow.
stretch has got to be the best pirate i've ever seen.

stretch is deaf
but stretch huddles near my guitar when i play

stretch seems to find the vibrations relaxing.
stretch likes music. he's never heard it
but he doesn't know music is supposed to be heard.

stretch has a pair of fangs that'd rattle a sabertooth's self-image, causing it to
spiral into existential angst it can't quite understand and copes with by posting
paranoid ramblings on facebook
stretch likes to show off his teefers when he's excited
stretch has never brandished his teefers in anger.
stretch is sworn to a vow of pacifism.
stretch is bound by treaty not to declare war on his humans for 20 years.
stretch is a prolific hunter of hair ties and headphones.
stretch is up to date on his licenses and supports conservation efforts.
stretch's white whale is a red dot.

stretch likes to sleep perfectly in sync with the fibonacci sequence.
the mathematical perfection of his nautilus whirl has baffled scientists and
inspired legions of tool cover bands.

stretch insists those he loves call him stretchy.
stretch is mr. stretch to those whose guts he hates.
stretch is rarely referred to formally because he is incapable of hatred.

stretch hates nail clippers.
stretch keeps his weapons secured behind 1 cm of toe bean alloy.
stretch hopes he never has to use them on anyone, but having the option
makes him feel safer. stretch does not dread home invasions.

stretch daydreams of home invasions so he can meet new strangers and anoint
them into his service.

stretch requires prompt 7 a.m. wet food deliveries. tardiness is not tolerated.
stretch demands a full bowl topped off with refrigerated filtered water. if he
runs out, he will not drink it until there is more on top.

stretch vomits competitively.

stretch wakes up from deep slumber to immediately tongue himself.
stretch licks his fur like he's in an on-sight rivalry with his own body and uses
outdated terminology to describe beating someone up.

stretch loves taking naps with his mom
stretch snuggles right into her arms
stretch loves
stretch is

stretch is a piece of my soul,
stretch is his mother's world.
stretch is a small act of kindness at the day's lowest point, repeated infinitely
both unexpected and reliable
in the exact proportions needed
stretch understands without hearing
stretch talks without speaking
stretch is, not was
in us

stretch will be.

my cat's deathbed

i.
the guitar stays on the floor.
i can't be alone
but all i want to do is be loud
the only space i can take up is sacred
he's the only one who won't hear.

last year barely exists
kept alive by fleeting memories, like scraps of leftover dream
my journal is full of
pages that have multiple months written on them
repeated, empty promises

the most thorough records, what reminds me best
that i've lived and these days and weeks and months
happened are the open tabs on my phone,
little windows to whims
and evenings where certain curiosities took over
i see the chords to a sad song
and a guide for xenoblade chronicles 2
and i know exactly when they were opened
the week(s?) we spent lost and gone
in disbelief our boy was leaving
hoping something, anything miraculous
would keep him around.

all it took for me to believe in snake oil was
the look on our cat's face
when he knew he was dying.

ii.
2022 killed so many memories
or at least holds them hostage.
i wish i remember the words we chose
instead of just the conversations.
there are fights i can't recall the cause of
but when i hold your hand and lose myself
in purple-red and hazel and white
i'm thankful i do not want to forget.

crying is really healthy, actually

when the well runs dry
you cannot squeeze water out of a smile,
no matter how rational it seems
that we are made of moisture.

part iv.

credits

roll. the list of names and
roles scroll past
everything that made this
what it was. each shot
taken, each cut endured.
but this is not the end.
the cameras are rolling
until the batteries
die.

post-credit scene

we sing songs of the world's end
and wait for it to burn
our story of inaction.

they say life is a marathon, not a sprint
in that they'd be right
because after our hard work is done
our hearts explode
26 miles in
destination reached
journey forgotten

it ends badly for all of us

i.
after an hour of wikipedia
reading about clockwork and
automata, venus rover concepts
the long now and the rosetta stone
it occurs to me just how little
anything i do matters
to anyone i know or don't
how impermanent our existence is
as individuals (what a concept)
or a species
with more languages dead than
alive
how can we live forever?
time
has burned our library
over and over again,
immemorial.

ii.
i think of the old man's
calm, assured existence
his notes to her
buried in *the snow leopard*
about the meaning of life
being reproduction
and the comfort he finds
in knowing from then on
he was playing with god's house money
existing full even while half empty
content at sail and at work
lighting a cigarette not out of compulsion
but of joy, asserting his age
and right to kill himself
any way he chooses.

the white

in between sips of stale
coffee i hear nervous shouts
of copy that needs to be checked
and papers shuffling, keys unlocking
words. the air bright with
purpose, shining on white desks.
the day is hard
but we never believed
this was easy.
my eyes fix on
the white
and
ease is relative
a relative of sloth
a disease that turns
ease to twilight action
easing back in a
chair until it
falls.

i think back to the night
i found inspiration
in an empty red bull can
and an empty mind
while snow filled an empty lot in
front of me.
the bed wasn't made and neither
was the work
i stayed for the work
but strayed from the work
wrote instead.
my throat felt full
with the swell of sleep
deprivation and
caffeine and
sugar and
my leg shook.
my leg shakes.
i'm shaken back

to the present
wondering how i present
myself. i look down
into the white.
my mug is empty.
i need to take
my headphones off
they're constricting me. i'm hung on
their coil, dreading the voices
but my deadline is tonight
and work is done easier here
than on wood in the dead
of moonlight
lying with red bull
in the snow.
i fix my eyes
on the white and
turn the keys

the theme, in a nutshell

i.
i fear my pain is a balloon
bouncing just out of reach
held by a string,
never too far away.
i fear letting go
i will watch it fly
free
and fall without its air.

ii.
yesterday,
or the day before,
i decided to fix my posture.
pulling a string
above my head
to straighten my
tired body,
i found myself much taller
than i ever thought
i was.

sisyphus is happy

the mountain is gone
long since ground
down,
eroded.

the land lies barren
open
dead.
the path is free

so he pushes
and smiles.
the boulder gives
gently

saying goodbye to karma

i.
the nigh-weekly hour and a half drive
from saginaw to lake orion
was often existential torture
a dull, repetitive slog
between my dirty dishes
and my friends and family.
one preferably trekked in the morning
with the comfort of frozen sugar
and hot fast food breakfast.
that friday evening, crying and shaking
i knew i would never forgive myself
if i didn't summon the energy to make the drive
that night.
i hated it dearly
it took everything i had to stand up

she warned me karma
should be remembered how she was
and i don't need to see her how she is.
she had seen better days.
happier places to pee on the floor.
her yells were not grouchy,
they were desperate. haunting
cries for love, any love
to hold her. her belly swollen
with some unknown malice.
i cried into her fur.
she contorted, trying to find her mother
where was she? where was she?
i remembered stretch the day
we said goodbye
and he needed, clung to life with everything
he had to be with her until the end.

mom placed karma on the air mattress and
snuggled next to her grumpy, infuriating
sweet and loyal lap cat
for the last time.

she went gently into the night.

ii.
i wasn't sure finnegan understood
but he had to.
life was different now, different than he'd ever known it.

i was always a cat person
but he was… perfection
from pup to ornery senior
just love incarnate
so smart and so, so dumb
a neurotic, whiny mess
who needs to be touched at all times
and can't stand hardwood floors.

i think we see ourselves in him.
like us, he always had her
never knew life without her.
he has perfected the art of the sad side eye
and always pouts like he's never been loved
in his entire life.

lately, he's tired.

you're not allowed to get old,
i always tell him.
it's illegal.
yet he keeps breaking the law,
repeat offender.
i wonder if he knows
it's only a matter of time
before he sees her again.

love, part ii: lowercase

hard to believe
people used to write
about healthy relationships.
something about discontent
really brings out that content.
we're suckers for heartbreak
easing loneliness with
self-destruction
addicted to the aesthetic
of lowercase letters.

i set out to write about you, love.
but when I think of you,
words fail and i smile.
you deserve brilliant sonnets
and properly capitalized
love letters
for no one's eyes
but yours

coindependent

i'm going to miss you so much,
i say,
over the next 24 hours.
your lip implodes in exaggerated sadness.
22 hours, i say, checking the math again.

...fine, 21 and a half.
...fine, 21.

i miss you within 30 minutes.

~

your arms were once 3 hours away,
every other weekend
while the world collapsed around us
the week when the highway was empty
felt like you lived next door.

now i wake up
to a dream.
my everything no longer worlds apart
your aura calms me,
your presence perfects me.
a day without you is a moonless night

trust the process

i often war with myself,
wanting to make things
afraid of bearing
my soul to anyone but
a page or a keyboard.

it's not very fun,
only being capable of originality
between 2 and 4:04 am
under a blood moon
after a week of rest
after a shitty month

but any given day
trading an hour of sleep
for having created anything
is a fucking steal.

it's a fleecing on par with ruth for cash
it's fire from olympus,
fruit from the garden.

to the poets i know, or knew

thank you for bleeding
onto a page and sending it through the mail.
soaked and bound,
your life
inkset. your lost loves
your regrets and reasons
your traumas and coping
mechanisms
the little joys and hatreds that catalyze
your mind, one in billions
to become. a small-g god amongst a universe
of white,
speaking existence.

thank you for sharing your courage.

now boarding

two months i've been away
my pens lost in a luggage compartment
shipped to a faraway place
i had no intention of visiting
luckily, you
have more than enough
and lent me
a few
for the road. the page
clean i go
forth, forging a new path through familiar surroundings.
i'll draw butterflies
with my tongue
as ink spills from my
klutzy metaphors
and grass rolls like toy balls
outside the frosted window.
my back stiffens, no hope of sleep.
but i think i'm in love
with the music of the rails
rumbling softly beneath
my feet.

Riley Murdock is a writer working from home in Auburn Hills, Michigan. Riley graduated from Michigan State University in 2019 with a bachelor's degree in journalism, and started working full-time in Saginaw later that year. Writing for a living makes it harder to write for fun, but poetry helps him stay grounded and process a never-stopping, ever-changing world. He has slowly learned to find inspiration in joy.

Riley lives with his wife Cristina and their fur babies Moose, Salem, and Oatmeal. He is passionate about shelter cats, the Detroit Tigers, playing instruments (none well) and singing just a bit too loudly—even when he's not sure that no one is listening.

Milton Keynes UK
Ingram Content Group UK Ltd.
UKHW040712031224
452051UK00006B/134